Homes for Everyone

Jennifer B. Gillis

Rourke
Publishing LLC
Vero Beach, Florida 32964

www.rourkepublishing.com

PHOTO CREDITS: © David Rose: cover; © Ed Endicott: page 4; © Dale Taylor: page 8; © Malcolm Rumnin: page 12; © Kenny Chi: page 14; © Todd Taulman: page 15; © Danny Bailey: page 17; © Jill Fromer: page 18; © Laurie Bell: page 19; © Sean Locke: page 20

Editor: Robert Stengard-Olliges

Cover design by Nicola Stratford

Library of Congress Cataloging-in-Publication Data

Gillis, Jennifer Blizin, 1950-
  Homes for everyone / Jennifer B. Gillis.
      p. cm. -- (My neighborhood)
    ISBN 1-60044-201-3 (hardcover)
    ISBN 1-59515-558-9 (softcover)
  1. Dwellings--Juvenile literature. I. Title.
  GT172.G555 2007
  392.3'6--dc22
                                    2006022165

Printed in the USA

CG/CG

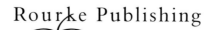

Rourke Publishing

www.rourkepublishing.com – sales@rourkepublishing.com
Post Office Box 3328, Vero Beach, FL 32964

Table of Contents

All Kinds of Homes

There are many kinds of homes. There are homes that can move around.

There are homes in the city that hold many people.
There are other homes made of logs or clay!

House

This house is a **single-family home**. It is for one family to live in.

A house like this can have many rooms. It has three bedrooms, a kitchen, and two bathrooms.

Apartment Building

Many families can live in an apartment building. Each apartment is a home.

An apartment has a few rooms. It has a kitchen and a bathroom.

Townhouse

A townhouse is like a single-family home. It is like an apartment, too!

Each townhouse is for one family. But many families live in this row of townhouses.

Mobile Home

Most homes stay in one place. **Mobile** homes can be moved by a truck!

A mobile home is for one family. It has bedrooms, a kitchen, and a bathroom.

Houseboat

A houseboat is a home that floats. Inside there are bedrooms and bathrooms.

Some families live on sailboats all year. Other sailboats are just for vacations.

Log Home

Some homes are made from things nearby. This is a log home.

People make log homes from trees. Parts of trees are stacked up to make walls.

Adobe Home

People build **adobe** homes where there are few trees.
Adobe homes stay cool in hot, dry weather.

Wet clay and straw makes adobe. The clay dries and stays hard.

Temporary Homes

Some homes are used for only a short time. These tents are **temporary** homes.

These are temporary homes too. People will stay here while their real homes are being **rebuilt**.

Unusual Homes

Sometimes people build unusual homes. This house was built in a tree.

Glossary

adobe (uh DOH bee) — bulding material made from wet clay and straw and dried in the sun

mobile (MOH buhl) — able to be moved from place to place

rebuild (ree BILD) — to build again something that was destroyed

single-family home (SING guhl FAM uh lee HOME) — home that is built to hold one family

temporary (TEM puh rer ee) — to last only for a short time

Index

FURTHER READING

Doering, Amanda. *Homes Around the World ABC*.
    Capstone Press, 2005.

Rosenthal, Betsy. *My House is Singing*. Harcourt, 2004.

Waters, Jennifer. *Right at Home*. Compass Point Books, 2003.

WEBSITES TO VISIT

en.wikipedia.org/wiki/List_of_house_types

ABOUT THE AUTHOR

Jennifer B. Gillis is an author and editor of nonfiction books and poetry for children. A graduate of Gilford College in North Carolina, she has taught foreign language and social studies in North Carolina, Virginia, and Illinois.